A CHOICE DROP OF

HONEY

FROM THE

ROCK OF CHRIST

THOMAS WILCOX

FREE GRACE PRESS

A Choice Drop of Honey from the Rock of Christ
by Thomas Wilcox (1621–1687)

Modernization and arrangement
copyrighted © 2020 by Jeffrey D. Johnson

Published by
Free Grace Press
1076 Harkrider
Conway, AR 72032

Cover design by Scott Schaller
Scottschallerdesigns.com

ISBN: 978-1-95259-902-6

A CHOICE DROP OF

HONEY

FROM THE

ROCK OF CHRIST

THOMAS WILCOX

Contents

Introduction

Thomas Wilcox (1621–1687) was a seventeenth-century Particular Baptist who should not be forgotten. The traits that marked the lives of other notable Baptists, such as John Bunyan and Benjamin Keach, marked the life of Thomas Wilcox.

Thomas was committed to the doctrine of *sola gratia*. Thomas viewed himself as a sinner in need of grace from start to finish. *Grace, grace, God's grace* was the theme of his life. Thomas claimed: "We must not bring anything to Christ. Not a penny of nature's highest improvements will pass in heaven. Grace will not stand with works." He was dependent upon a grace that is free, sovereign, and unmerited.

Thomas was committed to the doctrine of *sola fide*. Thomas understood that justification was by faith alone. Not by works of righteousness, Thomas often stated, but by faith alone is a sinner made right before God. It is not he who works, but he who believes that will be saved.

Thomas was committed to the doctrine of *sola Christus*. He stated: "When Satan charges sin upon your conscience, then for the soul to charge it upon Christ— that is, the gospel—that is to make Him Christ. He serves for that use. To accept Christ's righteousness alone, His blood alone for salvation, that is the sum of the gospel. When the soul, in all duties and distresses, can say, 'Nothing but Christ, Christ alone, for righteousness, justification, redemption.'" And what seems to be most notable about Wilcox is his high view of Christ, which provided him a low view of self. He saw his unworthiness in the light of Christ's righteousness. The righteousness of Christ was his only hope of salvation, and such a hope undergirded all Wilcox's pastoral and writing ministries.

Thomas was committed to the doctrine of *sola Scriptura*. And such a commitment led to an unyielding stance for the freedom of conscience and religious liberty. In the face of great opposition, Thomas fought for the purity of church worship and paid the price for living out his convictions. The Baptist historian

Thomas Crosby recorded that Thomas Wilcox was "two or three times put into Newgate (prison) for nonconformity."[1] He would rather be imprisoned than go against his conscience.

Finally, Thomas was committed to the doctrine of *soli deo gloria*. Though he was imprisoned by the Queen of England, Elisabeth I, he refrained from trusting in anything other than the imputed righteousness of Christ that comes by faith. He made much of Christ and little of himself and his sufferings. He lived a holy and pious life but only took comfort in Christ alone. He died, May 17, 1687, boasting only in one thing—his Savior.

Some sixty-five years earlier, Thomas was born, in 1621, in the small village of Lyndon, Rutland, about seventy-five miles due north of London. In the course of time, Thomas moved to London where he became the pastor of a small Baptist congregation that met in his home on Cannon Street.

Though he was firm and unyielding in his convictions, he was of a friendly and agreeable spirit.

[1] Thomas Crosby, *The History of the English Baptists* (London: John Robinson, J. Hodges, and A. Ward), 1740, 3:101.

He stood strong when he needed to stand up for the purity of the faith, yet he was amenable otherwise, for it is reported by Crosby that he "frequently preached among the Presbyterians and Independents."[2]

After the Great Plague of 1665, Thomas became the pastor of a Particular Baptist church that met in a small wooden house on Three Cranes Alley, Tooley Street in the Borough of Southwark. There he appears to have served out the rest of his ministry until his death.

With such a faithful ministry, Thomas is best remembered for a wonderful little book, the book you now hold in your hands, that he wrote before the Great Fire of London in 1666. This little book, *A Choice Drop of Honey from the Rock Christ*, has gone through many editions and translations. Though a small book, it has been greatly used by God throughout the centuries.

One notable account of how God used this little book is recorded by Thomas Crosby. About twenty years after the death of Thomas Wilcox, in the early eighteenth century, *The Choice Drop* came into the hands of a farmer living in central Finland—a man named Paavo Ruotsalainen. Though as a young man

[2] Crosby, *The History of the English Baptists*, 3:101.

Ruotsalainen had read his Bible through multiple times, he never found peace. This restlessness continued until he was given Wilcox's little book, *The Choice Drop*.

The Lord not only saved Ruotsalainen, but soon called him into the ministry. His newfound peace ignited a burning fire within his heart to preach the gospel to anyone who would listen. While maintaining his farm, he took the time to travel all over Finland to share the gospel. It is reported by Crosby that if all the miles of his evangelistic journeys were tallied it would be equivalent to a voyage around the world.

And Ruotsalainen never forgot Wilcox's little book. In reference to *The Choice Drop*, he warned professing Christians not only to begin with full dependence on Christ's righteousness but maintain that dependence. To forget that we can do nothing to gain justification before God was to move away from the gospel. Or, as Ruotsalainen often stated, "You started on your way with honey, but now have pitch and tar for food."[3]

---

[3] Crosby, *The History of the English Baptists*, 3:101.

Ruotsalainen's well-worn Bible has been preserved in Aholansaari, which is the farm in Nilsia where he lived out the rest of his life. There, inscribed in his Bible, are these words: "In this book lies the secret and kernel of the whole of life, and no one, neither the good nor the clever can know or understand this great and precious secret when his eyes have not been opened to his own wretchedness."[4]

Ruotsalainen was committed to this truth, and his commitment was greatly used by God to reach Finland with the gospel. Through his labors, God raised up many generations of believers, preachers, and churches.

The little seed sown by Thomas Wilcox in this little book, *A Choice Drop of Honey from the Rock Christ*, bloomed into a tree whose branches reached all of England. And soon the branches crossed the English Channel into all the rest of Europe and the world.

And though it has been reprinted throughout the centuries, it has fallen out of print in our day. Thus, it is our pleasure to bring this treasure back into circulation.

---

[4] Crosby, *The History of the English Baptists*, 3:101.

We have modernized the language, broken up the paragraphs, and added chapter divisions.

Working through this book, line by line, has been a great encouragement to me. I have been edified and my faith strengthened. I was often stunned, however, by the boldness of his language. For such clarity, directness, and boldness, I believe this is one of the best presentations of the gospel I have read.

I believe this book needs to be read by all. It is an ideal book to give to those who don't sense their depravity and hopelessness. This is the perfect antidote to pride and self-righteousness. May the Lord use this book to sound the alarm for sleeping sinners who remain comfortable in their slumber.

It would be even better to give this book to those who think they are saved but are not in reality. This includes many in our day. It may be that our parents and brothers and sisters and aunts and uncles and co-workers and friends fall into this category. I assume that all of us know a host of people who need their empty profession challenged, and this is a great book to do just that.

This is an excellent resource to hand to those who are fully aware of their sins and know they need salvation. *A Choice Drop* by Wilcox provides the remedy for those who are struggling to find peace for their souls. Wilcox shows us how to lay down our good works and surrender everything, not just all of our sins, to Christ. We must come to Christ not with our righteousness, but with our filthy rags. According to Wilcox, this is the hard part—giving up any pretense of self-worth. There is peace to be found in Christ; however, we have nothing to offer God but our sins.

For those who are saved but struggling with assurance, I know of no better book to give them than this one. Faith is not a feeling; faith is not faith in faith itself. Rather, faith is looking away from self to Christ. To have assurance, one must have a clear understanding of the gospel. The more we can grasp that salvation is all of Christ and nothing of self, the more we can rest in the unmovable Rock of Ages, for He alone is sufficient to save us from our sins.

For those who have assurance of their salvation, this book will be a wonderful encouragement to press on in the faith. It is good to be reminded of the preciousness of Christ. The just shall live, and continue to live, by faith alone in the finished work of Christ alone. This book zooms into the gospel and magnifies the depth of its beauty.

This is a great book for everyone. It can be read in one sitting, and it has something to offer every reader. I can't recommend it enough, and I hope that this little book and its author, Thomas Wilcox, will not be forgotten in our generation.

—Jeffrey D. Johnson

Conway, AR

To the Reader

I find in this latter day the love of the Lord shining in some measure, with its pleasant beams in my heart, warming my affections and enflaming my soul to not only love my Savior, whose transcendent love surpasses knowledge (Eph. 3:19), but also to love and wish well to all Zion's heaven-born children.

I find in this day many poor souls tossed to and fro, ready to be carried away with every wind of doctrine, by the slight of men and cunning craftiness, whereby they lay in wait to deceive (Eph. 4:14).

For this reason, there are many foundations to build upon that are false, upon which much labor is spent in vain. Because men are not speaking the truth in love, they are not growing up into Him in all things, who is the Head, even Christ (Eph. 4:15). There cannot be a growing in Christ without a union in Christ. And without a union in Christ, all that we do is cursed.

You will find, gentle reader, in this ensuing little treatise—if God is pleased to bless the reading of it unto you—the Lord saying, this is the way, walk in it. Turn not to the right hand or to the left hand. The way of being justified before God is in and through the righteousness of Jesus Christ. All our self-righteousness is as filthy rags, for surely shall one say, "In the Lord shall all the seed of Israel be justified and shall glory" (Isa. 45:24–25). It is only through the death of the Just One that the unjust ones are brought to God. As it is written, "He that knew no sin was made sin for us, that we, who were nothing but sin, might be made the righteousness of God in him" (2 Cor. 5:21).

Christian reader, let all that is of old Adam in you fall down at the foot of Christ. He only must have the preeminence. All the vessels of this spiritual new covenant-temple, from the cups to the pitchers, must all be hung upon Christ. He is to bear the glory. He, by His Father's appointment, is the foundation stone, the cornerstone, and the top stone. He is the Father's fullness of grace and glory. Whatever you need, you may come to Him; there is balsam in Him fit for the cure.

Dear reader, may the good Lord help you to experience this ensuing word of advice so that I may be made by God unto you like honey, sweet to the soul and healthy to your bones, and so that my soul shall rejoice with you.

Your brother in the faith and fellowship of the gospel.

T. W.

1

To Us All

A word of advice to my own heart and yours. If you are a professor of the Christian faith and partaker of all the ordinances of the church, you do well, for they are glorious privileges. But if you have not the blood of Christ at the root of your profession, then your profession will wither and prove only to be a cheap decorative suit to wear as you enter into hell.

If you retain guilt and self-righteousness under your profession, those vipers will eat out all the vitals of it. Try and examine, with the greatest strictness every day, what foundation your profession and hope of your glory is built on, see if your hope was laid by the hand of Christ. If not, it will never be able to endure the storm which must come against it. Satan will throw it all down, and great will be the fall of it (Matt. 7:27).

Glorious professor, you shall be winnowed. Every vein of your profession will be tried. It would be terrible to have it all tumble down and to find nothing solid for it to rest upon.

Soaring professor, see to your waxen wings, which will melt with the heat of temptations. What a misery it is to endure for a while to only crash down in the end with no foundation laid for eternity in your soul.

Gifted professor, make sure there is not a worm at the root of your confidence, which will spoil all your faith and make it die about you in the day of searching. Look over your soul daily and ask, "Where is the blood of Christ to be seen upon my soul? What righteousness is it that I stand upon to be saved?" Many eminent professors have come at length to cry out, in the sight of the ruin of all their duties, *Undone, undone to all eternity!*

Consider that the greatest sins may be hiding under the greatest duties and under the greatest terrors. Make sure that the wound that sin has made in your soul is perfectly cured by *the blood of Christ* rather than being skinned over with Christian duties, humblings, and enlargements.

Apply what you will, besides *the blood of Christ*, and it will poison the sore. You will find that you can't mortify sin truly if you have never seen Christ bleeding for you on the cross. Nothing can kill it but the beholding of Christ's righteousness.

Nature can afford no medicine that can cure the sickness of the soul. Healing from duty and not from Christ is the most desperate disease. Our poor ragged nature, even with all the highest improvements, can never spin a garment fine enough (without spot) to cover the soul's nakedness. Nothing can fit the soul for that use but Christ's perfect righteousness.

Whatever is of nature's spinning must be unraveled and set aside before the righteousness of

Christ can be put on. Whatsoever is of nature's putting on, Satan will come and plunder it away and leave the soul naked and open to the wrath of God. All that nature can do is not enough to drum up the least amount of grace. Nature, even in its best state, can never mortify sin or look Christ in the face.

Though you may be a professor who continues to hear, pray, and receive, you may remain miserable. Look about you; did you ever see Christ in distinction from all your own excellencies and righteousness? Has ever bit of self-confidence fallen away at the sight of the majesty of His love and grace (Isa. 2:17)?

If you have truly seen Christ, you have seen pure grace and pure righteousness—such infinite grace and righteousness that far exceeds all sin and misery. If you have seen Christ, you can trample upon all other forms of so-called righteousness of men and angels, for only Christ's righteousness is able to bring you into acceptance with God.

If you have seen Christ, then you would not attempt to obey God without the righteousness of Christ covering your imperfections for ten thousand worlds (1 Cor. 2:2). If ever you have seen Christ, you saw Him as a *Rock* higher than self-righteousness, Satan, and sin (Ps. 61:2). If you have seen Christ, this *Rock* continues to follow you (1 Cor. 10:4), and there will be a continual dropping of honey and grace out of that *Rock* to satisfy you (Ps. 81:16).

2

To the Examiner

Examine, if ever you have beheld Christ as the only begotten of the Father, full of grace and truth (John 1:14–17). Be sure you have come to Christ, that you have answered His call to your soul. Make sure you have been justified by Him.

Men talk bravely of believing what is true, but very few know what is true. Christ is the mystery of the Scripture; and grace is the mystery of Christ. Believing is the most wonderful thing in the world. Add anything of your own to it and you will spoil it. Christ will not so much as look at it. When you believe and come to Christ, you must leave behind your own righteousness and bring nothing but sin (Oh, that is hard!). You must leave behind all your holiness, sanctification, duties, humblings, and bring nothing but your wants and miseries—or else Christ is not fit for you or you fit for Christ. Bring anything but sin to Christ, and Christ will be a pure Redeemer and Mediator. Bring anything but sin to Christ and you will remain a sinner before Christ. It is the hardest thing in the world to take Christ alone for righteousness; that is, to acknowledge Him as Christ. Join anything of your own to Him, and you "un-Christ" Him.

When you go to God for acceptance, whatever comes in besides Christ, call it *antichrist*; bid it goodbye. Make only Christ's righteousness triumphant. All besides the righteousness of Christ is Babylon, which must fall (Isa. 1:10–12). Christ alone did tread the winepress, and there was none with Him (Isa. 63:3). If you join anything to Christ, Christ will trample upon it in fury and anger, and stain his raiment with the blood thereof.

Do you think it is easy to believe? Was ever your faith tried with an hour of temptations and a thorough sight of sin? Was it ever put to grapple with Satan and the wrath of God lying upon the conscience?

When you were in the mouth of hell and the grave, then did God show you Christ, a ransom. Then could you say, *Oh! I see grace enough in Christ.* If so, you may say that which is the biggest word in the world, "you believe." Untried faith is uncertain faith.

3

To the Believer

To the believing, you must go on with a clear conviction of sin, and the merits of the blood of Christ, and of Christ's willingness to save upon this one consideration that you are a sinner (something harder than making a world). All the power in nature cannot get so high, in a storm of sin and guilt, as to believe there is a willingness in Christ to save.

When Satan charges sin upon your conscience, then for the soul to charge it upon Christ—that is the gospel—that is to make Him Christ. He serves for that use. To accept Christ's righteousness alone, His blood alone for salvation, that is the sum of the gospel. Then the soul, in all duties and distresses, can say, "Nothing but Christ, Christ alone, for righteousness, justification, redemption" (1 Cor. 1:30). No humblings, no duties, and no graces can lift the soul above the reach of the billows.

All temptations, all Satan's advantages, and all our complainings are laid in self-righteousness and self-excellency. God pursues these by setting Satan upon you, as Laban pursued Jacob for his idols. These must be torn from you. These hinder Christ from coming in. Until Christ comes in, guilt will not go out. Where guilt is, there is the hardness of heart. Therefore, much guilt argues little, if anything, of Christ.

When guilt is raised up, take heed of seeking to relieve it any way but by Christ's blood. Otherwise, you will only become hardened. Make Christ, not your duties, your peace (Eph. 2:14). You may destroy Christ by duties as well as by sins. Look at Christ and do as much as you will. Stand with all your weight upon Christ's righteousness. Take heed of having one foot on your own righteousness and another foot on Christ's righteousness. Until Christ comes and sits upon a throne of grace in your conscience, there is nothing but guilt, terrors, secret suspicions, and the soul hanging between hope and fear, which is an ungospel-like state.

He that fails to see sin's utmost vileness and the utmost hell of his own heart will view the merits of Christ with suspicion. Be careful to not be such a great sinner (1 John 2:1). Try Christ as your advocate and you will find Him to be Jesus Christ the righteous. In all your doubting, fears, and storms of conscience, look at Christ continually.

Do not argue it with Satan, he desires that. Rather, bid him go to Christ, and He will answer him. It is His office to be our advocate (1 John 2:1). His office is to answer the law as our Surety (Heb. 7:22). His office is to answer justice as our Mediator (Gal. 3:20, 1 Tim. 2:5). And He is sworn to that office (Heb. 7:20). Put Christ upon it. If you will do anything yourself, as satisfaction for sin, you renounce Christ the righteous, who was made sin for you (2 Cor. 5:21).

Though Satan may seek to corrupt Scripture, he cannot answer Scripture. It is Christ's word that is the authority. Christ foiled Satan with it (Matt. 4:10). In all of Scripture there is not an ill word against a poor sinner who is stripped of self-righteousness. No, it points out that such a man to be the subject of the grace of the gospel and nothing else.

Believe that Christ is willing and that will make you willing. If you find you cannot believe, remember it is Christ's work to make you believe. Put Him upon it, for He works to will and to do of His good pleasure (Phil. 2:13). Mourn your unbelief, which is the setting up of guilt in the conscience above Christ and undervaluing the merits of Christ and accounting His blood an unholy, common, and unsatisfying thing.

You complain much about yourself. Yet, does your sin make you look more at Christ and less at yourself? That is right; your complaining is hypocrisy. To be looking at your duties, graces, and enlargements when you should be looking at

Christ—now that's pitiful. Looking at your performance will make you proud, while looking at Christ's grace will make you humble. By grace, you are saved (Eph. 2:5, 8).

In all your temptations, be not discouraged (James 1:2). Maybe those surges are designed not to drown you, but to heave you off yourself and onto Christ the Rock. You may be brought low, even to the brink of hell, ready to tumble into the abyss. You cannot be brought lower than the belly of hell. Many saints have been there, even doused in hell. Yet, there you may cry. There you may look toward the holy temple (Jonah 2:4) that was built with human hands, which none was able to enter without being purified and having an offering (Acts 21:26). But now Christ is our temple, our sacrifice, our altar, and our high priest, to whom none can come but sinners, and that without any offering but His own blood once offered (Heb. 7:27).

The greatest sinner did never surpass the grace of Christ. Do not despair. Hope still. When the clouds are blackest, even then look towards Christ, the standing pillar of the Father's love and grace, set up in heaven for all sinners to gaze upon continually. Whatever Satan or conscience may say, do not conclude against yourself. Christ shall have the last word. He is the judge of the living and the dead, and He must pronounce the final sentence. His blood speaks reconciliations (1 Cor. 1:20), cleansing (1 John 1:7), purchase (Acts 20:28), redemption (1 Peter 1:18–19), purging (Heb. 10:19), remission (Heb. 10:20), liberty (Heb. 10:19), justification (Rom. 5:9), and nearness to God (Eph. 2:18).

Not a drop of His blood shall be lost. Stand and listen to what God will say, for He will speak peace to His people that they return no more to folly (Ps. 85:8). He speaks grace, mercy, and peace (2 Tim. 1:2). That is the language of the Father and the language of Christ. Wait for Christ's appearing as the morning star (Rev. 22:6). He shall come as certainly as the morning, as refreshing as the rain (Hos. 6:3).

Do not for one moment take your eyes off of Christ. Look not upon sin but look first on Christ. When you mourn about your sin, if you do not see Christ, then away with it (Zech. 12:10). In every duty look at Christ. Before duty, look to Christ to pardon. In the midst of carrying out your duty, look to Christ to assist. And after completing your duty, look to Christ to accept. Without this, it is but carnal, careless duty.

Do not legalize the gospel, as if part of the gospel remained for you to do and suffer. This makes Christ but a half-mediator—as if you must bear part of your own sin and make part satisfaction. Let sin break your heart, but not your hope in the gospel.

Look more at justification than sanctification. In the highest commands consider Christ. Look at Him not as an exactor that requires, but as a giver who has undertaken the work on your behalf. If you have looked at your resolutions, endeavors, workings, duties, and qualifications more than at the merits of Christ, it will cost you dearly. No wonder you go about complaining that graces may be evidence. However, the merits of Christ alone, without them, must be the only foundation of your hope (1 Cor. 1:27). When we come to God, we must bring nothing but Christ with us. Any ingredients, or any previous qualifications of our own, will poison and corrupt faith. He that builds upon duties and graces knows not the merits of Christ.

This makes believing so hard, so hard, so far above nature. If you believe, then you must every day renounce (as dung and dross, Phil. 3:7–8) your privileges, your obedience, your baptism, your sanctification, your duties, your graces, your tears, your meltings, and your humblings, for nothing but Christ must be held up. Every day your working and your self-sufficiency must be destroyed.

You come empty-handed and take all out of God's hand, for Christ is the gift of God (John 3:16, 4:10). Faith is the gift of God (Eph. 2:8). Pardon is a free gift (Rom. 5:16). Ah! how nature storms, frets, rages at this—all is a free gift. Nothing can be purchased by our actions, tears, and duties, for all workings are excluded and are of no value in heaven.

If nature had contrived the way of salvation, it would have put it into the hands of saints and angels to sell it than into the hands of Christ, who gives freely. Because nature would set up a way to purchase by doing, it abominates the merits of Christ as the most destructive thing to it. Nature would do anything to be saved rather than go to Christ. Though Christ will have nothing, the soul would thrust something of its own upon Christ. Here is the great controversy.

Consider, therefore, have you ever seen the merits of Christ and the infinite satisfaction made by His death? Have you seen this when the burden of sin and the wrath of God lay heavy on your conscience? That is grace! The greatness of Christ's merits is not known but to the poor soul in deep distress. Slight convictions will have but a slight appreciation of Christ's blood and merits.

4

To the Sinner

Despairing sinner! You look to your right and left hand, saying, "Who will show us any good?" You are fretting over all your duties to patch enough righteousness together to save you. Look at Christ now; "look to Him and be saved, all the ends of the earth" (Isa. 19:22). There is none else. He is a Savior, and there is none beside Him (Isa. 19:21). Look anywhere else, and you will remain undone. God will look at nothing but Christ, and you must look at nothing but Christ.

Christ is lifted up on high, as the brazen serpent in the wilderness, that sinners at the ends of the earth, the greatest distance, may see and look toward Him (John 3:14–15). The smallest glance at

Him will be enough to save you. The slightest touch will bring healing to you. And God intends that you should look on Him, for He has set Him on a high throne of glory, in the open view of all sinners.

You have infinite reason to look on Him, no reason at all to not look on Him. He is meek and lowly of heart (Matt. 11:29). He has done that which He requires of His creatures (such as bearing infirmities (Rom. 15:1). He did not please Himself (Rom. 15:2). He will restore with the same spirit of meekness and bear your burdens (Gal. 6:2). He will forgive not only seven times but seventy times seven (Matt. 28:21–22).

Because we see sin as difficult to forgive, we think Christ sees it as difficult to forgive. Yet, we measure infinite love by our own standard and infinite merits with our own sin, which is the greatest pride and blasphemy (Ps. 103:11–12; Isa. 40:15). Hear what He says, "I have found a ransom" (Job 33:24). "In Him, I am well pleased" (Matt. 3:17). God will have nothing else. Nothing else will do you good, or clear your conscience, but Christ, who satisfied the Father. God does all on account of Christ. You deserve hell, wrath, and rejection; Christ deserves life and acceptance. He will not only show you the one, but He will give you the other. Christ is happy to pardon.

Consider that while Christ was on earth, He was more among publicans and sinners than among Scribes and Pharisees. The Scribes and Pharisees were His professed adversaries, for they were self-righteous. And though He is now in glory, He is attending to the needs of poor sinners. No! He has the same heart now in heaven as He did then. He is God, and He changes not.

He is the Lamb of God that takes away the sins of the world (John 1:29). He went through all your temptations, dejections, sorrows, desertions, and rejections (Matt. 4:3–12, 26; Mark 15:34; Luke 22:44; Matt. 26:38). He has drunk the bitterest of the cup and left you the sweet part—the condemnation is out. Christ drunk up all the

Father's wrath at one dose; nothing but salvation is left for you.

You say you can't believe; you can't repent—this only makes you more fit for Christ, for you have nothing but sin and misery. Go to Christ with all your remorselessness and unbelief to get faith and repentance from Him. Tell Christ, "Lord, I have brought not righteousness, no grace to be accepted in or justified by; I am come to receive your righteousness—I must have it."

We must not bring anything to Christ. Not a penny of nature's highest improvements will pass in heaven. Grace will not stand with works (Titus 3:4, Rom. 11:6). That is a terrible point to nature, which cannot think of being stripped of all self-worth—not having a rag of duty or righteousness left to display. Self-righteousness and self-sufficiency are the darlings of nature which she preserves as her life. That makes Christ seem ugly to nature. Nature cannot desire Him. He is just opposite to all nature's glorious interests.

Let nature but make a gospel, and it would make it quite contrary to Christ. It would be to the just, the innocent, and the holy. But the gospel of Christ is only for the sinner, the ungodly, the unrighteous, and the accused. Nature cannot endure the thought of the gospel being only for sinners; it will rather choose to despair than to go to Christ on such terms. When nature is confronted with its guilt and God's wrath, it will go to its old ways of self-righteousness. And infinite power must cast down those strongholds. Sadly, the self-justifier excludes himself from the gospel. Christ will look at the most abominable sinner before He looks at a self-righteous person. This is because Christ cannot be made justification, for he is no sinner.

To say, "I am a sinner," is easy. But to pray with the publican indeed, "Lord, be merciful unto me a sinner," is the hardest prayer in the world. It is easy to say, "I believe in Christ." But to see Christ full of grace and truth, of whose fullness you may receive grace for grace, that is the hard saying. It is easy to profess Him with the mouth, but to confess Him with the heart (as Peter confessed Him to be the Christ, the Son of the living God) is above flesh and blood.

Many call Christ "Savior," but few know Him as Savior. To see grace and salvation in Christ is the greatest sight in the world. None can do that, without, at the same time, seeing that His glory and salvation is theirs.

I may be ashamed to think, in the midst of my profession, that I have known little of the blood of Christ, which is the main thing of the gospel. A Christless, formal profession is the blackest sight next to hell. You may have many good things, and yet one thing may be lacking, which may cause you to go away sorrowful from Christ. You have not sold all that you have, never parted with all your own righteousness. You may be high in duty, and yet a perfect enemy and adversary to Christ in every prayer and in every ordinance.

Labor after sanctification to your utmost; but don't think sanctification can save you. If so, it must come down one way or another. Christ's infinite satisfaction, not your sanctification, must be your justification before God. When the Lord shall appear terrible out of His holy place, fire shall consume that as hay and stubble.

Sound religion is "to rest all upon the everlasting mountains of God's love and grace in Christ, to live continually in the sight of Christ's infinite righteousness and merits (they are sanctifying, without them the heart is carnal). In the sight of Christ's righteousness, you not only see the extent of your vileness, you see the extent of God's full pardon.

With this you pray and hear—seeing your polluted self and all your weak performances accepted continually. With this you trample upon all your self-glories, righteousness, and privileges as abominable. With this you cast yourself continually on the righteousness of Christ only, rejoicing in the ruins of your own righteousness.

You rejoice in the spoiling of all your own excellencies so that Christ alone, as Mediator, may be exalted on His throne. You gladly mourn over all your duties (however glorious they may be) which were performed in the sight and sense of Christ's love. For, without the blood of Christ on the conscience, all duties are but dead service (Heb. 9:14).

5

To the
Self-Confident

Reliance on free will will be easily dismissed (as it is by Scripture) in the heart of him who has had any spiritual dealing with Jesus Christ—as to the application of His merits and subjection to His righteousness. Christ is in every way too magnificent for our poor natures to apprehend. Christ is so infinitely holy that nature cannot look to Him. So infinitely good, nature can never believe Him to be such when it lies under full sights of sin. Christ is too high and glorious for nature so much as to touch.

There must be a divine nature first put into the soul, to make it lay hold on Him who lies so infinitely beyond the sight or reach of nature. That Christ that natural free will can apprehend is but natural Christ of a man's own making, not the Father's Christ, not Jesus the Son of the living God, to whom none can come without the Father's drawing (John 6:44–45).

Search the Scriptures daily, as mines of gold, wherein the heart of Christ is laid. Watch against constitutional sins, see them in their vileness, and they shall never break out into act. Keep always a humble, empty, broken frame of heart. Be sensible of any spiritual miscarriage. Be observant of all inward workings, fit for the highest communications. Keep not guilt in the conscience but apply the blood of Christ immediately—God charges the sin and guilt upon you to make you look to Christ, as the brazen serpent.

Judge not Christ's love by providence, but by promise. Bless God for shaking off false foundations, and for any way whereby He keeps the soul awakened and looking after Christ. Better sicknesses and temptations than security and slightness.

A fighting spirit will turn into a profane spirit that will sin and pray too. If a fighting spirit is not rooted out of the heart by a constant and serious beholding of Christ in duties, it will grow stronger and more deadly by being under church ordinances.

Measure not your graces by other attainments, but by trials. Be serious and exact in duty, having the weight of it upon your heart. Be as much afraid of taking comfort from duties as from sin. Comfort from any hand but Christ is deadly. Be much in prayer, or you will never keep up much communion with God. As you are in your prayer-closet, so you will be in all other ordinances.

Consider not duties by high expressions, but by low frames, and the beholdings of Christ. Tremble at duties and gifts. It was the saying of a great saint, he was more afraid of his duties than his sins: the one often made him proud, the other always made him humble. Treasure up manifestations of Christ's love, for they make the heart low for Christ and too high for sin. Slight not the lowest and meanest evidence of grace. God may put you to make use of the lowest, as you think, which will then be worth a thousand worlds to you (1 John 3:14).

Be true to truth, but not turbulent and scornful. Restore the fallen; help them up again with all the tender mercies of Christ. Set the broken disjointed bones with the grace of the gospel. High professor, do not despise weak saints. You may come to wish to be in the condition of the weakest of them. Be faithful to other infirmities, but sensible of your own. Visit sickbeds and deserted souls, for they are excellent scholars in experience.

Abide in your calling. Be dutiful to all relations as to the Lord. Be content with little as to the Lord—little will serve. Think little of the earth and much of heaven. Think everyone better than yourself and live in a humble state of mind as one fit to be trampled upon by all saints. See the vanity of the world, and the consumption that is upon all things, and love nothing but Christ.

Mourn to see so little of Christ in the world, so few needing Him—trifles please them better. To a self-confident soul, Christ is but a fable, the Scriptures but a story. Mourn to think how many are under baptism and church order but not under grace. Prepare for the cross; welcome it, bear it triumphantly like Christ's cross through scoffs, mocking, jeers, contempt, and imprisonments. But see it to be Christ's cross, not your own.

Sin will hinder you from glorying in the cross of Christ. Omitting little truths against the light may breed hell in your conscience, as well as committing the greatest sins against the light. If you have been taken out of the belly of hell into Christ's bosom and made to sit among princes in the household of God, then oh! how you should live as a pattern of mercy! Redeemed, restored soul, what infinite sums do you owe Christ! With what singular frames must you walk and do every duty! On Sabbaths, what praising days, singing of hallelujahs should be to you! Church fellowship— what a heaven, a being with Christ and angels and the communion of the saints!

What a drawing the soul in eternal love, as a burial with Christ, when you die to all things besides Him. Be astonished and wonder every time you think of Christ! And when you see sin, look at Christ's grace, which did pardon it. And when you are proud, look at Christ's grace, which will humble and strike you down in the dust.

Remember Christ's time of love when you were naked (Ezek. 16:8–9). Remember that He chose you. With such considerations, how can you ever have a proud thought? Remember whose arms supported you from sinking and delivered you from the lowest part of hell (Ps. 86:13), and shout in the ears of angels and men, forever singing "Praise, praise, grace, grace" (Ps. 148).

Daily repent and pray; and walk in the sights of grace, as one that has anointings of grace upon you. Remember your sins and Christ's pardonings. Remember your deserts and Christ's merit. Remember your weakness and Christ's strength. Remember your pride and Christ's humility. Remember your many infirmities and Christ's restorings. Remember your guilt and Christ's new applications of His blood. Remember your failings and Christ's rising up. Remember your wants and Christ's fullness. Remember your temptations and Christ's tenderness. And remember your vileness and Christ's righteousness.

Blessed soul!—whom Christ shall find not having his own righteousness (Phil. 3:9) but having his robes washed and made white in the blood of the Lamb (Rev. 7:14).

Woeful, miserable professor! You have not the gospel within. Rest not in church trials; you may pass that and be cast away in Christ's day of trial. You may come to baptism and never come to Jesus and the blood of sprinkling (Heb. 12:24). Whatever workings or attainments, short of Christ's blood, merit righteousness (the main object of the gospel), fall short of the gospel, and leave the soul in a condition of doubt and questionings. And doubt, if not looked unto, will turn to a slightness of spirit, one of the most dangerous of frames.

Trifle not with ordinances. Be much in meditation and prayer. Wait diligently upon all hearing opportunities. We need doctrine, reproof, exhortation, consolation, as the tender herbs and grass has of the rain, the dew, the small rain, and the showers (Deut. 32:2). Do all you do as soul work unto Christ (Zech. 7:5–6) and as immediately dealing with Christ Jesus as if He were looking on you, and you on Him, and fetch all your strength from Him.

Observe what holy motions you find in your soul to duties. Prize the least good thought you have of Christ; the least good word you speak of Him sincerely from the heart. Rich mercy! Oh, bless God for it! Observe, if every day you have the Dayspring from on high, with His morning dews, constantly visiting you (Luke 1:78). Have you the bright Morning Star, with *fresh* influences of grace and peace, constantly arising (Rev. 22:16) and Christ sweetly greeting the soul in all duties? What duty makes not more spiritual will make more carnal. What does not quicken and humble will deaden and harden.

Judas may have the sop (the outward privilege of baptism), yet at the supper (the church-fellowship) it was *John* who leaned on Christ's bosom (John 13:23). That is the gospel-ordinance-posture, in which we shall pray, and hear, and perform all duties. Nothing but lying in that bosom will dissolve hardness of heart, and make you mourn kindly for sin. Only leaning on the bosom of Christ will cure a lackadaisical spirit, bring humility from within, make the soul cordial to Christ, make sin vile to your soul, and yea, transform the ugliest piece of hell into the glory of Christ.

Never think you are right as you ought to be, a Christian of any attainment, until you come to see and feel yourself lying in the bosom of Christ, who is in the bosom of His Father (John 1:18). Pray to the Father to see Christ in such a way. You can come with no request that pleases Him better. He gave Him out of His own bosom for that very end, to be held up before the eyes of all sinners as the everlasting monument of His Father's love.

Though looking at the natural sun weakens the eye, looking at Christ, the Sun of Righteousness, only strengthens the eye of faith. Look at Christ and you will love Him. Look at Christ and you will live. Think on Him continually. Keep your eye constantly upon Christ's blood, or temptation will shake you. If you will see sin's sinfulness, to loathe and mourn it, do not stand looking upon sin, but look first on the suffering of Christ. If you would see your graces and your sanctification, do not stand gazing upon them. Look at Christ's righteousness first (see the Son and you see all), and then at your graces in the second place.

What you believe in is that which becomes your hope. Go to Christ with your sin and misery, not with your graces and holiness. Have nothing to do with your graces and sanctification (they will but veil Christ) until you have seen Christ first. He that looks on Christ through his graces is like one that sees the sun while under water. Look on Christ only as shining in the firmament of the Father's love and grace, then you will see Him in His own glory, which is unspeakable.

Pride and unbelief will have you see something in yourself, but faith will have you see nothing but Christ, who is inexpressibly glorious. Christ must swallow up your sanctification as well as your sin— for God made Him both for us, and we must make Him both (1 Cor. 1:30; 2 Cor. 5:21).

He that sets up his sanctification to look upon and to comfort himself, sets up the greatest idol, which will strengthen his doubts and fears. Do not look off of Christ, or presently, like Peter, you will sink in doubts.

A Christian only lacks comfort when he breaks away from the order and method of the gospel, which is to look on his own righteousness before looking to Christ's perfect righteousness. This is to choose to live by candlelight rather than by the light of the sun. The honey that you draw out from your own righteousness will turn into perfect gall; and the light that you take from yourself will turn into a black night upon the soul.

Satan tempts you to walk about in your own grace, to comfort yourself with your own performance. Then the Father comes and points you to Christ (who is rich and glorious) and bids you to study His righteousness (and His bidding is an enabling). This is a blessed motion, a sweet whispering, and the great remedy to unbelief. Follow the least hint of such a bidding, seal it with much prayer, prize it as an invaluable jewel, and it will be an earnest of more to come.

Conclusion

Again, if you would pray and cannot, and if you find yourself discouraged, then see Christ praying for you—see His interest with the Father for you (John 14:16). If you be troubled, see Christ as your peace (Eph. 2:14)—see Christ as leaving His peace for you when He went up to heaven. Remember again and again Christ charging you not to be troubled—no, not in the least (sinfully troubled) so as to obstruct your comfort or your faith John 14:1, 27).

He is now upon the throne, and by suffering on the cross, in the lowest state of His humiliation, He has spoiled everything that can hurt or annoy you. He has borne all your sins, sorrows, troubles, temptations, and He has gone to prepare mansions for you.

You who have seen Christ as everything and yourself as nothing, are dead to all self-righteousness. Moreover, you are a Christian, one highly beloved, and who has found favor with God—a favorite of heaven.

Do Christ this one favor for all His love to you, love His poor saints and churches (the meanest and weakest—notwithstanding any difference in judgment), for they are engraved on His heart, as the names of the children of Israel on Aaron's breastplate (Ex. 23:21). Let them be so on your heart. Pray for the peace of Jerusalem, for they shall prosper that love you (Ps. 122:6).